CREATIVE COMPANIES

THE STORY OF APPLE

SARA GILBERT

JAICO PUBLISHING HOUSE

Ahmedabad Bangalore Bhopal Chennai
Delhi Hyderabad Kolkata Lucknow Mumbai

Published by Jaico Publishing House
A-2 Jash Chambers, 7-A Sir Phirozshah Mehta Road
Fort, Mumbai - 400 001
jaicopub@jaicobooks.com
www.jaicobooks.com

Published in arrangement with
The Creative Company
123 South Broad Street, Mankato, MN 56001, USA

To be sold only in India, Bangladesh, Bhutan,
Pakistan, Nepal, Sri Lanka and the Maldives.

Design by Zeno Design
Production by Christine Vanderbeek
Art Direction by Rita Marshall

Photographs by Alamy (Aerial Archives, Avatra Images, JoeFox,
Richard Levine), Corbis (Bettmann, Ed Kashi), Getty Images
(Apic, Apple, Jack Atley/Bloomberg, Alan Dejecacion/Newsmakers,
Andrew Harrer/Bloomberg, Kelsey McNeal/ABC, Miguel Medina/AFP,
Gilles Mingasson/Liaison, Tom Munnecke, SSPL, Justin Sullivan,
Ted Thai/Time & Life Pictures, Kim White/Bloomberg,
James D. Wilson/Liaison)

THE STORY OF APPLE
ISBN 978-81-8495-363-3

Jaico Print-on-Demand Edition: 2025

Page design and layouts: Special Effects, Mumbai

Printed by
Repro India Limited, Mumbai

CREATIVE COMPANIES

THE STORY OF APPLE

iPod

When Steve Wozniak designed a computer in 1976, his friend Steve Jobs suggested that they find a way to make it available to the public. Wozniak took the computer to his bosses at Hewlett-Packard to see if they were interested in producing it. They turned him down. Jobs approached his employers at Atari as well, offering them the opportunity to buy and market the computer, but again the idea was rejected. Instead of giving up, however, Wozniak sold his most prized possession—a Hewlett-Packard programmable calculator—for $250, and Jobs sold his beloved red-and-white Volkswagen bus for $1,500. They put the money together and started Apple Computer, Inc. in 1977. Over the next 30-plus years, that company would help revolutionize the computer industry.

1
Geeks and Geniuses

Steve Wozniak and Steve Jobs met in Cupertino, California, in the summer of 1971. They were introduced by a mutual friend who assumed that their shared love of electronics would lead to a lasting friendship.

The 21-year-old Wozniak had recently dropped out of college and built his first "computer," which had lights that blinked in response to certain commands. Jobs, who was 16, had also been tinkering with technology for class projects in high school. The two Steves quickly hit it off.

Starting that fall, Wozniak and Jobs found themselves working together frequently, either trying to hawk an electronic product that one of them had designed or dressing up as ***Alice in Wonderland*** characters to earn $3 an hour at a mall. In 1973, Wozniak landed his first full-time job, designing handheld calculators at Hewlett-Packard. Jobs, who dropped out after one semester at Reed College in Portland, Oregon, became employed as a technician at Atari, a video-game company.

Although they were both using their technical expertise in their jobs, Wozniak and Jobs still spent their spare time playing with electronics. In 1975, they joined the new Menlo Park-based Amateur Computer Users Group, also known as the Homebrew Computer Club, where hobbyists demonstrated their projects and shared ideas. Computers were becoming more widely used industrially, thanks to companies such as IBM and Xerox, and personal computers (PCs)—smaller machines designed to be used by one person at a time—were gaining interest as well. Many members of the Homebrew Computer Club were intrigued by the do-it-yourself computer kits advertised in ***Popular Electronics*** magazine, and Wozniak and Jobs were among those who dreamed of building their own computers. Jobs recognized that Wozniak was a more talented designer than he was and could create more complex systems, so he started focusing on the possibility of selling his friend's devices.

When Wozniak brought the basic design of a new computer to a Homebrew Computer Club meeting in February 1976, Jobs immediately recognized its potential for a mass market. It was built around a $20 microprocessor—the component that allows the computer to respond

Although short on formal education, Steve Jobs had an abundance of ambition as a young man to commands and powers its operations—and could be reproduced relatively easily for about $25. Jobs thought that they could sell the guts of Wozniak's design—just the printed circuit boards, without a case, keyboard, power supply, or monitor—to the hundreds of other hobbyists in the club for $50 each and make a nice profit.

That hadn't been part of Wozniak's plan. He was comfortable with the work he was doing and the decent $24,000 annual salary he was making at Hewlett-Packard. He had gotten married a few months earlier and was more interested in stability than in the uncertain enterprise of

The Apple I was sold as something of a kit, as users had to connect their own keyboards and screens selling personal computer components. Still, Jobs's suggestion sparked his interest. "It had never crossed my mind to sell computers," Wozniak said. "It was Steve who said, 'Let's hold them up in the air and sell a few.'"

Before they could do that, however, Wozniak was obligated by his contract with Hewlett-Packard to obtain a legal release from the company before producing and promoting his own electronics products. In the process of asking for the release, he and Jobs offered Hewlett-Packard the right to produce and market the computer. The company declined, as did Jobs's bosses at Atari. The only remaining option was to sell the computer design themselves.

Now all they needed was a name for their company. Although they considered such technical names as Executek and Matrix Electronics, its was

"In the end, I hope there's a little note somewhere that says I designed a good computer."

Steve Wozniak,
Founder of Apple

Apple was officially called Apple Computer, Inc. until 2007, when it became simply Apple Inc.

iPhon 3G S
The fastest, ost powerful
iPho yet

The original Apple

When Apple Computer was first incorporated, cofounder Ronald Wayne drew a logo for the company: a picture of Sir Isaac Newton sitting under an apple tree. By later in 1977, however, Steve Jobs had decided that wasn't the right look for Apple. He asked a friend who owned a public relations agency for help; that friend put art director Rob Janoff on the job. "The first thing I did was go to the supermarket, buy a bag of apples, and slice them up," Janoff said. "I just stared at the wedges for hours." Eventually, he came up with an idea: a black apple with a bite taken out of the right side. He presented the idea to Jobs, who liked everything but the color, or lack thereof. So Janoff striped the apple with the colors of the rainbow, in opposite order. That logo was used until 1997, when Jobs decided to use a solid "crystal white" apple instead.

Jobs's suggestion of Apple Computer, an idea that might have grown out of his experience working at an orchard in Oregon, that proved the winning choice. And when they took the completed computer to a Homebrew Computer Club meeting, they introduced it as the Apple I.

Their first customer, Paul Jay Terrell, was at the meeting that day. Terrell had opened the Byte Shop, one of the first computer retail store chains in the country, a year earlier. He was interested in the Apple and told Wozniak and Jobs to keep in touch. So the next day, Jobs showed up at Terrell's store in Mountain View, California, saying, "I'm keeping in touch." He left the shop with an order for 50 fully assembled computers, at $500 each.

Although they were elated to make such a huge sale, neither Wozniak nor Jobs had the funds necessary to buy all of the parts to build 50 complete computers. They secured a $5,000 loan from two of Wozniak's coworkers, then persuaded a local supplier to extend 30 days of credit on the rest of the parts. Jobs set up a workshop at his parents' home in Los Altos, California, and he, Wozniak, and a third partner who had been asked to help get the company off the ground, Ronald Wayne, worked feverishly to assemble the computers before they had to repay their supplier.

With a single day to spare, they delivered the first 50 Apples—basically just circuit boards stuffed with chips and processors—to the Byte Shop. Although Terrell had assumed that they would be delivering the computers in cases, with monitors, keyboards, and power supplies, he nonetheless paid them the $25,000 he had promised and then "finished" the computers himself. Approximately $17,000 of that money paid off the loan and the supplier, but the remaining $8,000 was Apple's first profit.

2
Building the Business

The profit from their first sale was enough to spur Jobs to look for more customers and to encourage Wozniak, who was still working at Hewlett-Packard, to spend his spare time improving the original design for the Apple I.

But their initial success wasn't enough to stop Wayne from fretting about the financial risks inherent in a start-up business. On April 12, 1976, Wayne accepted a one-time payment of $800 for his shares in the company and ended his relationship with Apple Computer.

Wayne's concerns were justified, as the company didn't have enough cash to continue building computers. When Wozniak finished tweaking the features of the original Apple, integrating revolutionary high-resolution graphics that allowed users to view up to six colors on the screen (the Apple I was in black-and-white only), he and Jobs both realized that the new computer, called the Apple II, would sell well. But each one would cost several hundred dollars to produce. "How do you build 1,000 of something that costs a lot of money?" Wozniak asked. "We didn't have any money."

While Wozniak tinkered with the technology, Jobs tried to drum up financial support for the business. He found it in Armas Clifford "Mike"

Markkula Jr., who had retired at age 32 after having made millions while working with computer processor developers Intel and Fairchild. Markkula recognized the potential in Jobs's ambition and Wozniak's brilliance, so he agreed to help create a business plan for Apple. He also invested more than $90,000 of his own money in the company and arranged another $250,000 in credit.

With that financial backing in place, Apple was officially incorporated on January 3, 1977. A month later, Markkula hired the company's first president, Michael Scott, who had worked with him at Fairchild. In April, the Apple II was released at a retail price of $1,298. Unlike its barebones predecessors, the Apple II had an attractive case, came with a standard keyboard and power supply, and could produce color graphics. Within 9 months, a total of 570 Apple IIs had been sold.

On the strength of those sales, the company grew. By 1980, 1,500 people worked at Apple's headquarters in Cupertino. As Wozniak worked on a new disk drive and started the Apple III, other

Joining Apple as an investor in 1977, Mike Markkula would remain a company executive until 1997

talented engineers at the company began developing new products, too. One team began building a computer named the Lisa in 1978, and another team started work on the Macintosh—named after project manager Jef Raskin's favorite type of apple, the McIntosh—in September 1979.

So great was Apple's commercial success that the owners decided to sell stock in Apple to outside investors. Shares were first offered to the public on December 12, 1980, and all 4.6 million sold out in minutes at a price of $22 apiece. By the end of the day, Apple was worth nearly $1.8 billion. Jobs, Wozniak, and Markkula, who each owned

"Apple's market share is bigger than BMW's or Mercedes's or Porsche's in the automotive market. What's wrong with being BMW or Mercedes?"

Steve Jobs,
CEO of Apple

Apple's headquarters are in Silicon Valley, the California region famous for its technology companies large quantities of stock in the company, suddenly had millions of dollars each. More than 40 other Apple employees also became millionaires that day, thanks to the stock options that were part of their compensation packages.

Such wealth changed the nature of the business for Wozniak. He became more interested in spending his riches than in focusing on product development. In February 1981, he and his girlfriend (his marriage had ended in 1980) decided to fly to San Diego in the Beechcraft Bonanza airplane he had bought. During takeoff, the plane stalled and plummeted to the ground, bouncing through two fences and coming to a stop in an embankment. Wozniak suffered amnesia, temporarily losing his short-term memory. After a five-week recovery, he decided to take a part-time leave of absence from Apple.

Wozniak wasn't the only one departing from the company; on February 25, 1981, Scott fired 40 employees and killed several unproductive hardware projects. A month later, he resigned, saying he was no longer having fun at Apple. Markkula took over as president, while Jobs, who had been heading up the Macintosh division, became chairman of the board.

In 1983, a new president and chief executive officer (CEO) joined the company: John Sculley, who was lured away from PepsiCo with a $500,000 salary, another $500,000 in bonuses, a $1-million signing bonus, and stock options. Around the same time, the much-anticipated Lisa—larger in both size and storage capacity than the Apple III—was released. The next year, a slimmed-down Lisa 2 was introduced. Both Lisas tanked; they were notoriously slow and too costly for most business consumers. The line was discontinued in 1985, and thousands of unsold Lisas were buried in a landfill four years later.

In January 1984, Apple Computer introduced the Macintosh, or Mac—a user-friendly desktop computer. Unlike earlier computers, which required users to type commands using a specific computer "language," the Mac featured graphical user interface (GUI) capabilities, which meant that it was controlled by a mouse-driven pointer or arrow that clicked on icons, or pictures on the screen. GUI elevated the Macintosh above competition from other companies making PCs, such as Commodore and Tandy, and helped the line exceed early expectations. Within 100 days of its release, more than 72,000 Macs had been sold. "We could have sold 200,000 Macintoshes," product marketing manager Barbara Koalkin told *USA Today,* "if we could have built them."

The Macintosh was the first mainstream computer to offer "point-and-click" mouse operation

space invaders

The forgotten founder

Steve Jobs and Steve Wozniak didn't start Apple alone. Before they even began building the original Apple, they asked Ronald Wayne, a video-game draftsman at Atari who had worked with Jobs, to join them. Wayne was almost 20 years older than the other 2 and had already run an engineering business of his own. Jobs offered him a 10 percent cut in any profits that Apple made, which was enough to entice Wayne to join the venture. Wayne designed the company's first logo and stayed up nights working on plans for the business. But less than two weeks after Apple was officially founded, he decided that he wanted out and gave up his interest in the company. He walked away and never looked back—even when Apple made millions. "I have never had the slightest pang of regret," Wayne said. "I made the best decision with the information available to me at the time."

3
Falling Apples

The Macintosh was a success, but the company was struggling. Wozniak, who had returned in 1982, was disappointed by the focus being placed on the Mac instead of his pet project, the Apple II. Although he had been assigned to develop new technology for the Apple II, including reconfiguring the Mac's improved mouse to work for it, he felt adrift within the company. Early in 1985, Wozniak walked away from Apple for good.

Meanwhile, Jobs had decided that Sculley lacked vision for Apple's future. Sculley, however, thought that Jobs was meddling in areas where he didn't belong. In April 1985, he asked the board of directors for permission to eliminate Jobs's operational roles, which they did. But before Sculley could deliver the news to Jobs, Jobs learned of the decision and planned to oust Sculley instead. Sculley was warned of Jobs's intentions and immediately stripped him of everything but the title of chairman—a figurehead position without any power. On September 17, 1985, Jobs resigned and left to start another computer company of his own, called NeXT.

Without Jobs to distract him, Sculley embarked on a mission to ramp up sales figures for Apple products—especially the Mac, whose sales had slowed since its release. Among the many advancements made during the mid-1980s, two in particular led to a surge in sales. The first was pairing the Mac with Apple's LaserWriter printer and Aldus PageMaker software, which made desktop publishing easy and accessible. The other breakthrough was the introduction of the Mac Plus, which had more ROM (read-only memory, which stores permanent data) than the original version and one megabyte of RAM (random-access memory, which stores temporary data), which could be expanded to four megabytes if the user so chose.

Sculley's dedication to product development and marketing led to tremendous growth in sales during his tenure at Apple (1983–93). Sales increased from $600 million in 1983 to almost $8 billion a decade later. But despite those impressive numbers, not everything Sculley touched turned to gold.

One of the biggest flops under his reign was the Mac Portable, the company's first attempt at a laptop. Shortly after the Mac was released in 1984, Apple announced its intention to shrink the computer to the size of a book. Five years later, it introduced the Mac Portable with a full-size keyboard, speakers, and the largest, clearest flat

Steve Jobs, John Sculley, and Steve Wozniak (left to right) in 1984, shortly before they parted ways screen available on a laptop—at a retail price of $5,799. But while competitors such as Toshiba and Zenith offered popular PC laptops (without the GUI technology that set Macs apart) that weighed fewer than 10 pounds (4.5 kg), the Mac Portable was a hefty 15.8 pounds (7.2 kg). Its size made it unwieldy for users to carry or use in small spaces, one of the main reasons it wasn't a strong seller for Apple. The slimmed-down PowerBook, first introduced in 1991 and promoted by retired basketball star Kareem Abdul-Jabbar, was much more popular with consumers. More than 400,000 PowerBooks sold within the first year, adding more than $1 bil-

Although the Mac Portable was heavy,
many buyers appreciated its user-friendly operating system

lion to Apple's revenues that year.

The problems with the Mac Portable led to a shakeup in the technological leadership at Apple that resulted in Sculley's appointing himself Chief Technology Officer (despite his lack of technological experience) in 1990. He immediately made launching the Newton MessagePad, a personal digital assistant (PDA), his priority. But the Newton, which took more than six years to create, was riddled with problems—including inconsistencies in the device's highly promoted handwriting recognition capabilities—and failed to take off as Sculley had hoped. His enthusiastic support of the Newton, which would be discontinued in 1998, raised questions about Sculley's leadership of the company.

At the same time that Sculley was promoting problematic products, he was also dealing with increasing competition in the PC market. Apple's biggest competitor was not actually another hardware manufacturer but software giant Microsoft, which had created Applesoft

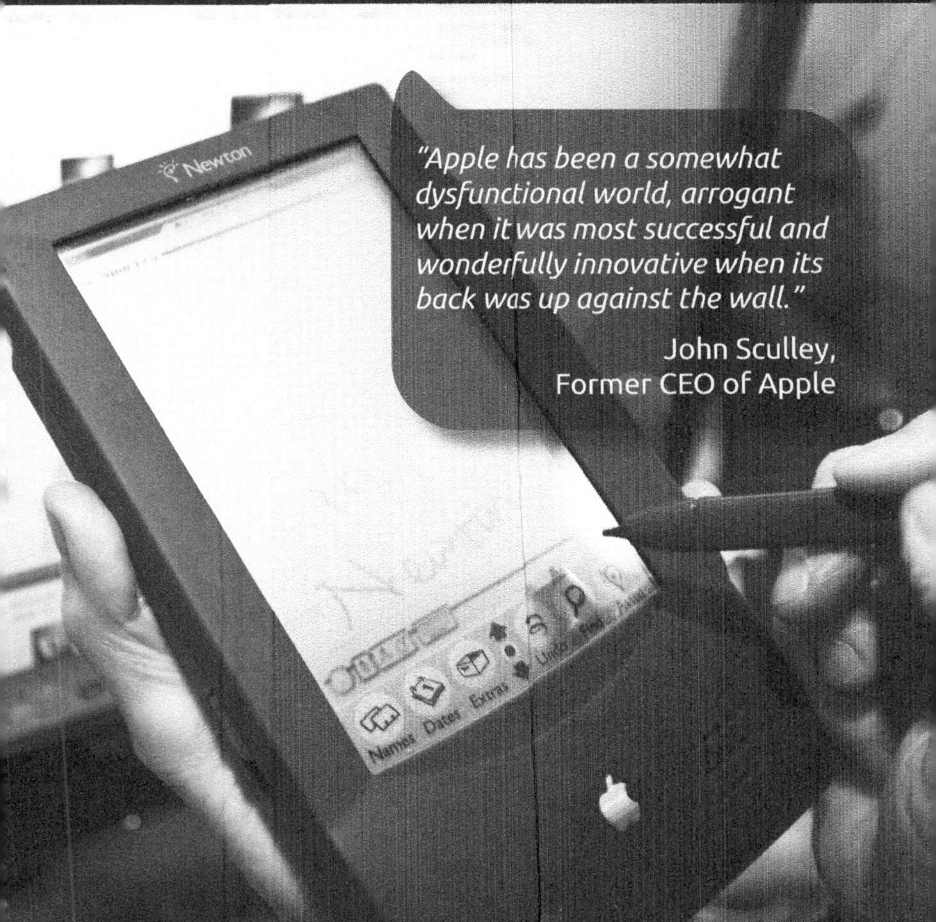

"Apple has been a somewhat dysfunctional world, arrogant when it was most successful and wonderfully innovative when its back was up against the wall."

John Sculley,
Former CEO of Apple

The Newton MessagePad represented
Apple's expansion beyond traditional computers and software

Where's Woz now?

When Steve Wozniak left Apple Computer, he had no intention of returning. And unlike cofounder Steve Jobs, he didn't. Instead, he finished his degree in electrical engineering and computer science at the University of California at Berkeley, put on two music festivals, and generously gave of both his time and money to help improve computing capabilities in schools. Wozniak has been involved in several business ventures, including his recent appointment as chief scientist for Fusion-io, a Salt Lake City-based technology company developing advanced storage options for computer users. But although he still loved tinkering with technology, Wozniak found other hobbies, too. In 2009, he was one of the celebrity competitors on the television show *Dancing with the Stars.* "I just thought it would be something different and unusual to do," said Wozniak, who admitted he had never danced before. "I'm just competing against myself and trying to have fun."

BASIC, the programming language for the Apple II, and had worked on software for the Macintosh as well. In 1985, Microsoft owner Bill Gates demanded that Apple halt development of its own programming language or lose its license on Applesoft BASIC. Sculley agreed to the request. Later that year, Gates insisted that he be allowed to use some Mac GUI technologies in exchange for the continued production of Mac software by Microsoft. Knowing that the software was necessary, Sculley signed that contract as well.

The decision would soon haunt him. In 1988, Microsoft released its Windows 2.03 operating system—the first Mac-like GUI application for PC. Apple sued. A judge ruled that all but 10 of the contested features were covered by the contract signed in 1985 and that Microsoft could continue to use them. Although Apple appealed the decision in a costly, seven-year legal battle, the courts upheld the original decision.

By 1992, Sculley had grown weary of the constant battle to remain ahead of the com-

petition and attempted to resign—but the board of directors asked him to stay on. A year later, however, the board lost confidence in his ability to lead the company. On June 18, 1993, Sculley stepped down as CEO but retained the figurehead title of chairman; 3 months later, when Apple posted a 97 percent drop in earnings for the fourth quarter, he resigned that position as well.

4

Back on the Jobs

The man who replaced Sculley was known as "The Diesel." Michael Spindler, who had started his career with Apple in 1980 as the marketing manager for the European arm of the company, had earned that nickname both for his large physical stature and his work ethic.

Spindler was known for working around the clock in order to solve a problem or meet a goal. That intensity would be a hallmark of his tenure as CEO as well.

When Spindler took over in 1993, Apple's global market share was rivaled only by PC maker IBM, and it was the most profitable computer company worldwide. But Spindler believed that Apple needed to reorganize in order to maintain its position at the top. He eliminated 2,500 jobs, slashed the research and development budget, and canned several projects.

Those changes helped bring about four consecutive quarters of strong growth. They also helped make the company more attractive for a potential merger with a larger company, which would give Apple more financial backing. But when IBM offered to pay $40 a share for Apple, Spindler rejected the deal. He turned down a lucrative offer from Sun Microsystems as well.

One of the reasons Spindler passed up these offers was that the 1994 release of the Power

Mac—a high-end computer targeted at the business community—had spurred a double-digit growth in sales. Based on the speedy PowerPC processer, the Power Mac had sold 1 million units in the first 10 months it was available. Spindler was confident that Apple's stock prices would rise, increasing the company's value, if he waited.

Spindler wasn't the only one waiting around at that time; hundreds of customers were anticipating the arrival of their computers as well. Apple's leadership team had underestimated sales growth late in 1994 and found itself unable to meet the demand for its products, particularly the high-end Power Macs, during the holiday rush. That disastrous holiday season led to a backlog that grew to almost 500,000 Macs by June.

Things got worse in 1995, when Apple's PowerBook 5300, the first laptop with a PowerPC processer, literally exploded. Just after Apple had shipped out the first 1,000 PowerBook 5300s to excited dealers, 2 units caught fire—one at an Apple programmer's house and the other at

As [illegible] Michael Spindler (pictured, right, with John Sculley)
[illegible]thered Apple's growth in the European market

a factory in Singapore. The notebooks were powered by lithium-ion batteries, which had overheated while charging and exploded. Apple quickly issued a recall, but its reputation was already badly burned.

So was Spindler's. In 1996, he was fired and replaced with board member Gilbert Amelio, who held 16 electronic and technological patents and a PhD in physics from the Georgia Institute of Technology. Despite the change of leadership, Apple celebrated its 20th anniversary in 1997 with combined losses of $740 million in the first 2 quarters, due largely to the costs of restructuring after approximately 2,800 layoffs. In the midst of that bad news,

Classrooms represented an enticing market for Apple
and other computer companies in the early 1990s

however, Amelio brokered a deal that would have a long-term impact on Apple's future, acquiring NeXT and bringing company founder Steve Jobs back to Apple as an adviser.

Jobs's responsibilities soon changed. On July 6, board member Edgar S. Woolard Jr. called Amelio at home and asked him to step down. Few people were surprised when Jobs was then asked to fill the vacant CEO role. Although he didn't accept the title, Jobs agreed to increase his involvement in the company until a new CEO was found.

One of Jobs's first moves upon his return was to ask several longtime board members to resign—including Markkula, who had been the one constant within the company since its beginning. Even more surprising, however, was Jobs's announcement that Apple had agreed to work cooperatively with Microsoft on software development. Jobs scolded the crowd at the Macworld Expo in Boston for booing the news. "Apple has to move beyond the point of view that

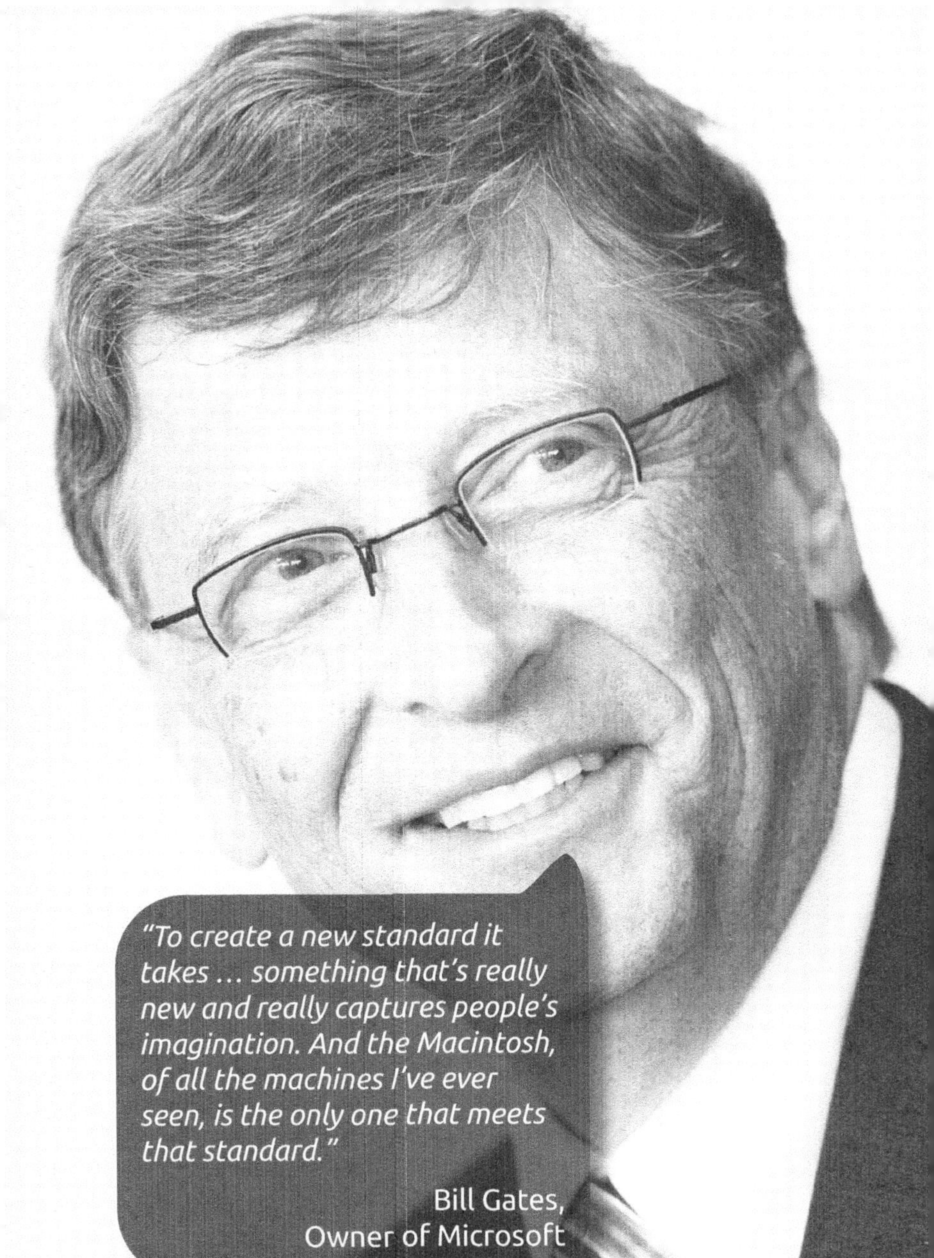

Apple had a complex relationship with Microsoft owner Bill Gates, who was both a rival and a partner

Importance of industrial design

Apple's iMac was the first desktop computer built without a floppy drive (a nod to the increasing importance of the Internet and the declining reliance on disks). It was also the first new Apple product in years with a consumer-friendly price—just $1,299. But its appearance received the most attention. The iMac broke the boring beige-box mold in which most computers had previously been packaged. The computer's rounded, translucent, candy-colored plastic case came courtesy of Jonathan Ive, the 32-year-old head of Apple's design team who went on to lead the design teams that created the titanium-clad PowerBook, as well as the iPod and the iPhone. Ive's work helped make Apple's products the benchmark by which other companies judged their product designs. His work also brought him the kind of attention that few industrial designers enjoy. "For a designer, there couldn't be a more exciting place to work at this moment than Apple," Ive said.

for Apple to win, Microsoft has to lose," he said.

Remarkably, Apple quickly began to win again. Jobs, now the interim CEO, made a series of decisions designed to return the company to profitability, including the 1997 launch of the online Apple Store, which offered customized Macs. The store received more than $12 million worth of orders in its first 30 days of operation. That same year, CompUSA agreed to dedicate separate space to Apple products within all 148 of its computer superstores in the United States. Bolstered by strong sales of both Mac's new, user-friendly, GUI-based operating system and the upgraded Power Mac, Jobs announced that Apple would make a profit in the first quarter of 1998.

The crowning achievement of Jobs's return was the release of the iMac G3 on May 6, 1998. Jobs had insisted that the company needed to offer a consumer product for less than $2,000 (the average price for PCs at the time was $1,300, but Apple did not have an inexpensive model in its line) and had given a small group of engineers the task of coming up with a "radically different" machine. The gumdrop-shaped iMac was packed with power, memory, and Internet capabilities. It was also beautifully designed in a translucent blue case—and cost only $1,299. Within 6 weeks, more than 278,000 iMacs were sold, making it the fastest-selling Macintosh model ever.

5
iSuccess for Apple

The success of the iMac kicked off a flurry of new and improved offerings from Apple, including the iBook laptop—basically an iMac flattened into laptop proportions—that sold as well as the iMac had. It also propelled Apple back into steady profitability.

The best news for Macintosh faithful came at the Macworld Expo on January 5, 2000, when Jobs ended his keynote address with a quick announcement. "I'm pleased to announce today that I'm going to drop the 'interim' title," he said. The crowd responded by chanting "Steve! Steve! Steve!" for several minutes.

Apple's board rewarded Jobs, who had taken no compensation while serving as interim CEO, with stock options for 10 million shares, which were worth $872 million at the time, and a Gulfstream V airplane that cost almost $88 million. "We are delighted to give him this airplane in appreciation of the great job he has done for our shareholders during this period," explained board member Edgar Woolard.

The economic downturn that began in 2000 led to a slump for Apple and the technology industry in general. Early in 2001, Apple posted its first quarterly loss since 1997. But that didn't stop the company from pushing forward. It opened 25 Apple Retail Stores across the country in

2001. In October, it also released a revolutionary product that would redefine its focus in the years to come—a portable media player called the iPod.

Unlike other MP3 players already available from manufacturers such as Sony, Samsung, and Philips, the five-gigabyte iPod was quick to load and could store approximately 1,000 CD-quality songs, as compared with approximately 500 in many other players. The first version worked only with Mac computers, but by 2002, new iPods also worked with Microsoft Windows operating systems. The product was so popular that by the middle of 2003, more than 1 million iPods had been sold.

Although the success of the iPod reduced Apple's reliance on its Macintosh products for revenue, the company remained committed to upgrading its computers as well. A completely redesigned iMac G4 with a 15-inch liquid crystal display (LCD), which provided a sharper picture than older monitors, was released in 2002, and 2 new PowerBook G4 models were introduced in 2003. Apple also premiered iLife—a software

A gifted speaker and salesman,
Steve Jobs oversaw an Apple renaissance after his 1996 return

package that made it easy to make and manage one's own movies, photos, and music—and unveiled its first Internet browser, Safari, that year. But its biggest venture was again musical: On April 28, Apple introduced the iTunes Store, where customers could purchase and download digital versions of more than 200,000 songs for $0.99 each.

For the iTunes Store, Apple secured the cooperation of the five largest recording companies in the world—BMG, EMI, Sony Music Entertainment, Universal, and Warner. Selling the songs themselves wouldn't help Apple make money; after paying royalties and transaction fees to the music companies, Apple would earn just a few cents for each song sold. But Apple hoped that the availability of songs on iTunes would lead to a jump in sales of iPods, the only device compatible with the music sold in the store. That strategy worked, and by 2009, more than 220 million iPods had been sold, easily making it the best-selling MP3 player on the market.

Between October 2001 and September 2010,
Apple released 22 different versions of the iPod

On the heels of the iPod phenomenon, Apple released the much-anticipated iPhone in January 2007. With a sleek design, multi-touch screen, Internet capabilities, and iPod-like music storage, the iPhone was immediately popular with cell phone users. Within 200 days of its release, Jobs announced that more than 4 million units had been sold worldwide.

Apple's flurry of innovation under Jobs's leadership had changed the financial fortunes of the company. Between 2003 and 2006, the price of Apple's stock had increased from $6 per share to about $80 per share. The success of the iPod and the iPhone helped stock prices top $200 by the end of 2009.

The only bad news to come out of Apple's Cupertino headquarters was Jobs's announcement in early 2009 that he would be taking a six-month leave of absence after being diagnosed with cancer. Jobs returned that fall, after a liver transplant, eager to get back to business. "I'm vertical, I'm back at Apple, loving every day of

"It's hard to remember what I did before the iPod. iPod is more than just a music player, it's an extension of your personality and a great way to take your favorite music with you everywhere you go."

Mary J. Blige,
Grammy Award-Winning Singer

Loaded with popular features such as Safari, iTunes, and YouTube, iPads were an instant hit in 2010

I'm a Mac

In 2006, Apple launched the "Get a Mac" ad campaign, which was designed to take direct aim at its biggest competition—PCs that run on the operating systems created by the software giant Microsoft. The ads, which featured young comedic actor Justin Long as a Mac and John Hodgman, an older comedian, as a PC, focused on the shortcomings of PCs as compared with Apples. In one, Hodgman is hosting a bake sale and tells Long that he is trying to raise money to solve the problems with Microsoft's latest Vista operating system. In another, Hodgman is in a wheelchair with bandaged appendages and has to explain that his injuries occurred when someone tripped over his power cord and pulled him off the desk—giving Long the opportunity to promote the magnetic power cords used with Apple's laptops. Microsoft responded in 2008 with an "I'm a PC" campaign of its own, in which its users proudly proclaim that they are PCs.

it, and I'm getting to work with our incredibly talented teams to come up with some great new products," he said in his first public appearance in September 2009. Among the products on the docket was the April 2010 release of the $499 iPad, a touch-screen tablet device that looked and responded much like a large iPhone. On its first day available, more than 300,000 iPads were sold. Jobs remained mum about future gadgets in the works, but Apple continued to upgrade and improve its operating system and core products. Unfortunately for the company, recurring health problems forced Jobs to take another leave of absence in January 2011.

In its 30-year history, Apple has become known as one of the most innovative companies in the world. It has enjoyed periods of unbelievable success and survived bouts of bad decision-making. It has set the standards for technological advancement, but it has also had to bury a few poorly made products. In the process, it has gone from a little-known company started by two computer hobbyists to an internationally recognized brand celebrated for its creativity and cutting-edge technology.

Glossary

board of directors a group of people in charge of making big decisions for a publicly owned company

circuit boards boards used in electronics that allow a device to perform specific functions

contract a legally binding agreement between two people or two parties

credit an arrangement that allows a buyer to obtain a product now and pay for it later, often with interest

desktop publishing the production of printed material from a printer linked to a desktop computer that uses software on the computer to create documents

digital recorded using a technique that converts sounds or pictures into electronic signals

economic having to do with the system of producing, distributing, and consuming goods within a society

executive a decision-making leader of a company, such as the president or chief executive officer (CEO)

gigabyte a unit of computer memory or data storage capacity equal to 1,024 megabytes, or 1 billion bytes (Apple desktop computer hard drives have 500 gigabytes to 2 terabytes)

incorporated formed a firm or company into a corporation by completing all of the required procedures and paperwork

interim serving in a position on a temporary basis, usually to fill in before a permanent replacement can be found

license to grant permission for the use of trademarked, patented, or other individually owned products or services

lithium-ion batteries rechargeable batteries used in many portable electronic devices that are composed of electrically charged particles of the lightweight metal lithium

market share the percentage of the total sales of a given type of product or service that is attributable to a particular company

merger the combining of two or more entities into one through a purchase or a pooling of interests

MP3 players computerized music players that support a digital audio format known as MP3

personal digital assistant a lightweight electronic device that looks like a hand-held computer but is designed to perform specific tasks, such as keeping track of schedules or serving as a diary or personal database

profit the amount of money that a business keeps after subtracting expenses from income

public relations the practice of establishing and maintaining a favorable connection between a company and the public

quarter one of four three-month intervals that together comprise the financial year; public companies must report certain data on a quarterly basis

royalties payments made for the use or sale of a copyrighted work, usually a percentage of the revenues obtained through the use or sale of the work

shares the equal parts a company may be divided into; shareholders each hold a certain number of shares, or a percentage, of the company

software the programs that run a computer, or tell it how to operate

stock shared ownership in a company by many people who buy shares, or portions, of stock, hoping the company will make a profit and the stock value will increase

stock options options for employees or investors in a company to buy or sell that company's stock; stock options are often given as part of an employee's benefits package

Selected Bibliography

Amelio, Gil, and William L. Simon. *On the Firing Line: My 500 Days at Apple.* New York: Harper Business, 1998.

The Apple Museum. "History." The Apple Museum. www.theapplemuseum.com.

Hormby, Tom. "Michael Spindler: The Peter Principle at Apple." *Low End Mac,* April 6, 2006. http://lowendmac.com/orchard/06/michael-spindler-apple.html.

Levy, Steven. *The Perfect Thing: How the iPod Shuffles Commerce, Culture, and Coolness.* New York: Simon & Schuster, 2006.

Linzmayer, Owen W. *Apple Confidential* 2.0: *The Definitive History of the World's Most Colorful Company.* San Francisco: No Starch Press, 2004.

Salter, Chuck. "100 Most Creative People in Business, #1 Jonathan Ive." Fast Company. http://www.fastcompany.com/100/2009/ jonathan-ive.

Young, Jeffrey. *Forbes Greatest Technology Stories: Inspiring Tales of Entrepreneurs and Inventors Who Revolutionized Modern Business.* New York: John Wiley & Sons, 1998.

Index

JAICO PUBLISHING HOUSE

Elevate Your Life. Transform Your World.

ESTABLISHED IN 1946, Jaico Publishing House is home to world-transforming authors such as Robin Sharma, Sadhguru, Osho, the Dalai Lama, Deepak Chopra, Eknath Easwaran, Paramhansa Yogananda, Devdutt Pattanaik, Radhakrishnan Pillai, Morgan Housel, Napoleon Hill, John Maxwell, Brian Tracy, and Stephen Hawking.

Our late founder Mr. Jaman Shah first established Jaico as a book distribution company. Sensing that independence was around the corner, he aptly named his company Jaico ('Jai' means victory in Hindi). In order to service the significant demand for affordable books in a developing nation, Mr. Shah initiated Jaico's own publications. Jaico was India's first publisher of paperback books in the English language.

While self-help; religion and philosophy; mind, body and spirit; and business titles form the cornerstone of our non-fiction list, we publish an exciting range of current affairs, history, biography, art and architecture, travel, and popular science books as well. Our renewed focus on popular fiction is evident in our new titles by a host of fresh young talent from India and abroad.

Jaico's translations division publishes select bestselling titles in over 10 regional languages including Gujarati, Hindi, Kannada, Malayalam, Marathi, Tamil, and Telugu. These include titles from renowned national and international authors like Sudha Murthy, Gaur Gopal Das, Swami Mukundananda, Jay Shetty, Simon Sinek, Ankur Warikoo and Jeff Keller.

Visit our Website

Boasting one of India's largest book distribution networks, Jaico has its headquarters in Mumbai, with branches in Ahmedabad, Bangalore, Chennai, Delhi, Hyderabad, and Kolkata. This network ensures that our books reach all parts of the country, both urban and rural.